JUAN FEARFUL'S
First Day at School

Dr. Mac and Dr. Anaida
Illustrations by Marco

Print information available on the last page

Rev. date: 01/03/2018

To order additional copies of this book, contact:
Xlibris
1-888-795-4274
www.Xlibris.com
Orders@Xlibris.com

Introduction for Teachers and Parents

A child's mind is wonderful and imaginative, but at times their imagination is accompanied by fear. With the help of parents and teachers, we can help our children lessen their fears with stories like this one. Note that the top section is for read aloud, and the kids can follow in the simpler section written below.

Juan Fearful was 5 years old and afraid of many things. *"¡Tengo miedo!"* he would say. At night his mother had to check under his bed and in his closet for scary monsters with big sharp teeth.

Juan Fearful was afraid of many things.

Tomorrow will be Juan's first day at school. He is going to enter kindergarten. He is excited about going, but he is also afraid. Mother tries to make him feel better by saying that he is becoming a big boy, *"¡Qué niño grande!"*

Juan is a big boy. He is going to kindergarten. He is afraid of his new school.

Today Juan and his mother went to the store to get ready for school. His mother bought him new shoes, pants, a shirt, a lunch box and a bright red backpack with a car on it. *"¡Qué bonito!"* But he couldn't stop feeling afraid.

Juan's mother bought him new things for school. But Juan was still afraid.

Last year he had gone to Baby Bunker's Day Care Center, but now he was going to a new school. He will have a new teacher. Juan missed his old school, but especially his old friends. *"¡Mis amigos!"*

Juan missed his old school. He missed his old friends.

Juan tried not to worry about it anymore. He wanted to have fun today. He played all day with his toy cars and trucks. He loved his cars and trucks. He had big ones, and small ones, red, yellow and green ones. He had fire trucks, police cars, racing cars, pickup trucks and construction trucks. *"¡Qué muchos juguetes!"*

When he played with his toy cars and trucks, he forgot about school.

After dinner he took a bath and got ready for bed. He jumped under the covers. And Fluffy, his cat jumped in after him. Mother checked the room for monsters, read him a story, and kissed him goodnight. Juan quickly went to sleep. *"¡Buenas noches!"*

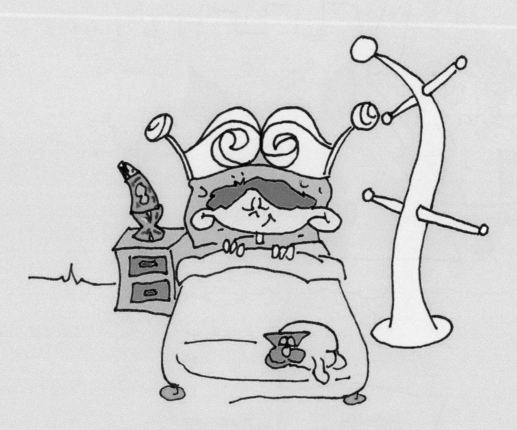

Juan took a bath and went to sleep.

That night, Juan Fearful dreamed about his first day of school. He saw himself walking to school. The school looked like a big castle, but it was dark and ugly. When he came close to the school the principal jumped out. She was a big mean giant with a gigantic ruler. *"¡Qué miedo!"*

Juan Fearful had scary dreams. In his dreams the school was an ugly castle and the principal was big and mean.

And, when Juan entered the classroom in his dreams, the teacher looked angry and she yelled a lot. The room was painted strange colors with giant tables and chairs. The children were very big and scary. All their heads turned to stare at Juan. *"¡Ay, qué miedo tengo!"*

**The teacher looked angry in his dreams.
The children were scary too.**

When Juan's mother woke him up, he was sweating. "Mami, Mami, I don't want to go to school. *¡No quiero ir a la escuela!* Please don't make me go! It's scary. *¡Tengo miedo!*"

Mother calmed him down and told him everything would be okay. *"No te preocupes.* You have nothing to worry about, you'll be just fine", she said softly.

Then he told her about the horrible dream he had. "Don't worry," She said again, "It was a nightmare, *una pesadilla*. It was only make believe. Sometimes we have scary dreams when we are afraid."

"¡Qué bueno! Whew! Thank goodness," said Juan, as he took a long, deep breath.

Mother said, "*Juan, no te preocupes*, don't be afraid. It was a just a scary dream."

Feeling a little better, he washed his face, brushed his teeth, put on his new clothes, and went downstairs for breakfast. Mother made him his favorite breakfast of cereal with bananas and milk.

"*¿Qué te pasa*, Juan? Why didn't you eat your food?" asked his mother. "*No quiero comer*. I'm not hungry. I have a tummy ache," said Juan.

Juan liked breakfast. But, he did not eat. He felt sick. *"No quiero comer"*.

Juan's mother knew he was nervous, so she gave him a big hug and said, *"¡Te quiero mucho!"* She told him he was going to have a great day. But Juan was still not too sure about that!

Mother gave Juan a great big hug.

Juan started school at 8 o'clock in the morning, so he and his mother left early to school. It took only ten minutes for them to walk to the new school but it seemed far away. *"¡Qué lejos!"*

Juan and his mother walked to the new school.

When Juan and his mother finally got to school, he was very surprised. The school was not dark, scary and tall like a castle. It was a small, bright and pretty building! *"¡Qué bonita es la escuelita!"*

Juan and his mother got to school.
The school was not scary!

Juan's mother opened the school door. His heart pounded so hard it seemed to come out of his chest. His lips trembled and he started to sweat. He felt like butterflies were fluttering inside his stomach. He was afraid. *"¡Tengo miedo!"*

Mother opened the school door. Juan was very afraid. *"¡Tengo miedo!"*

On the way to his classroom, Juan and his mother bumped into a small woman with a friendly, happy face and a very pretty smile. "Why hello!" she said with a chuckle. "I'm Miss Little, the new principal. Who are you?"

Juan was amazed. She was nothing like the giant in his dreams! *"Me llamo Juan",* he said quietly.

"Bienvenido," said Miss Little. You belong in Room 4.

Juan was surprised that Miss Little spoke Spanish. Juan and his mother continued on their way to Juan's classroom.

Juan met the principal. She was not mean!

Juan stood in front of his classroom and wondered what would be on the other side of the door. The door had a sign on it. Mother read it to him, "It says, Welcome to Room 4. That means *¡Bienvenidos!*"

As his mother was about to open the door, Juan felt like running away. When his mother opened the classroom door, Juan was even more surprised than before!

**Juan walked into the classroom.
He was very surprised!**

The room was bright with pretty pictures on the walls. The classroom had two buckets of toy cars and trucks to play with during recess. All the tables and chairs were made small, just like Juan. He was very surprised! *"Juguetes?"*

Juan saw the classroom. There were toy cars and trucks! He was very surprised.

In the corner, there was a man in a big funny tie that made Juan laugh. When he saw Juan, he walked over and shook Juan's hand. "Why hello there, you must be Juan. *Soy Maestro Bob,* your new bilingual teacher."

Juan was surprised and asked. "How do you know my name?" "I know all my students' names!" said Mr. Bob. "Wow!" thought Juan, "I like my new teacher!"

Juan met his teacher. He liked his new *maestro!*

When Juan looked around, he saw smiling faces. He saw Connie, José, Angela and all his old friends from Baby Bunker's Day Care. They had to go to kindergarten too! They were also in his new school! Juan was very happy. *"¡Estoy feliz!"*

Juan saw his old friends. They were in kindergarten too. He was happy!

Juan had been very fearful about school because sometimes we are afraid of new things. This made him have scary dreams.

But now he was very excited! He decided kindergarten was going to be lots of fun. He was glad to be in a new school! He was not afraid of school anymore.

"¡Ya no tengo miedo!"

Juan was happy. He was not afraid of school anymore!

Follow-up for read aloud

(A few days later...)

Every day in school Juan was learning something new. He was very happy, with his new school. On one beautiful day, Juan was practicing the alphabet, when Mr. Bob said, "Class, today we have a new student. Please say hello to Karisa." The whole class said, "Hi Karisa!"

Juan remembered how scared he was on his first day of school, so he went up to Karisa and said, *"Hola, me llamo Juan. Would you like to play with my friends and me?"* She smiled.

Juan learned that sometimes we are afraid of things that are new. But, he was happy to learn that new things can really be great.

"¡Estoy contento y aprendiendo mucho!"

About the authors:

DR. MAC was born and raised in New York City and presently lives in Orange, California with his wife. He is a retired school psychologist.

DR. ANAIDA was born in Puerto Rico and grew up in New York City. She is a professor at Chapman University. She presently lives with her husband Dr. Mac in Orange, California.

About the artist:

MARCO, the illustrator and our son, is currently a costume designer in Hollywood, California. He did this artwork when he was in high school.

Special thanks go to our daughter Karisa, who encouraged us to publish this book, and our nephew Brandon, who did the graphic design.

Printed in the United States
By Bookmasters